ORDER FORM

Meeting Procedure for Condominium and
Homeowner Associations
1st Ed. 1993 ____ @ $15.00 ea. __________

Postage, shipping, handling __________
One book $3.00
(Additional books, add $1 each postage and handling)
Missouri residents add sales tax __________
10% discount for members on orders of
$50 or more __________

Total enclosed: __________

(Make checks payable to National Association of Parliamentarians)

Name ____

Address ____

State ____________Zip Code________Phone______________

Organization ____

____

___Visa___Mastercard ___/___ Exp. Date
____-____-____-____ Credit Card Number
______________________________Signature
(___) ____ - __________ Phone number
($10 Minimum)

Mail to:
National Association of Parliamentarians
Publications Department
6601 Winchester Avenue, Suite 260
Kansas City, MO 64133-4657
or FAX to (816) 356-5605

Meeting Procedure

for

Condominium and Homeowner Associations

Joyce L. Stephens, PRP

for the
National Association of Parliamentarians
Education Committee
Kathryn C. Scheld, PRP, Chairman

6601 Winchester Avenue, Suite 260
Kansas City, MO 64133-4657
(816) 356-5604
FAX (816) 356-5605

*Meeting Procedure for Condominium and
Homeowner Associations*
Parliamentary procedure for boards and membership
meetings—based on *Robert's Rules of Order Newly Revised*

First edition, July 1993
ISBN 1-884048-00-5
Index.

Manufactured in the United States of America
by Graphic Arts Resources, Inc., Tampa, Florida

Introduction

"Developers sell dreams. Managers and board members are left to deal with the realities of people coming together in a form of joint ownership who are unprepared for community living and who have not accepted the principle that any form of community living will cause some sacrifice of individual rights." Jesslyn McBride, PCAM (Professional Community Association Manager), Executive Director, Suncoast Chapter, CAI (Community Associations Institute), in the publication, *Guide for Community Association Management (in Florida).*

Management of a community association is a challenge. The board of directors must deal directly with common property and the assessments and rules to maintain it. In addition, it is expected to keep the peace.

One of the major differences between community associations and other not-for-profit corporations is that the members of the corporation have a personal or business financial interest. Most are nonprofit, but some associations are for-profit corporations. Many condominiums are residential, but some are business or professional offices. This book will focus on the nonprofit associations.

The condominium or owners' association must abide by the statutes of the state in which it is incorporated. These statutes may include rules for condominium associations, homeowners' associations, mobile home associations, cooperatives and other forms of owners' associations.

The statutes may prescribe procedures for notice of meetings, posting of the agenda, elections, and the use of general and limited proxies. In addition, many states write administrative rules that must be followed for meetings. Otherwise, the responsibilities are generally the same as other nonprofit associations. Some states do not adopt regulations regarding these particular forms of associations, but adopt statutes for all corporations. The board of directors must be aware of the requirements in the state where they are operating.

The board of directors is responsible for preserving the assets of the corporation in an orderly and reasonable manner. The unit owners are responsible for electing the officers and directors who will manage the association, and for voting on amendments to the association documents.

The members are unit owners who have a substantial stake in the outcome of decisions made by the board of directors.

The board of directors should use proper parliamentary procedure to conduct meetings in a legal, productive, and timely manner. The board must be mindful of the rights of individuals in the association while making decisions that are in the best interests of the whole association community.

This book is designed to make the task of conducting meetings less complicated. The material contained in the book is basic parliamentary procedure that will help boards and officers with most procedures not covered by the bylaws and other documents. All procedures should be viewed in light of state and local statutes and ordinances.

J.L.S.

Contents

Index of motions

Order of Business

The Agenda

ORDER OF BUSINESS

The order of business given here is a suggested order. The board will choose the appropriate order of the business for meetings. For example, it is always good to hold an election early in the meeting, so that there will be time to count the ballots before adjournment.

1. Call to order
2. Certification of notice
3. Reading and approval of the minutes
4. Reports of officers, boards, and standing committees
5. Reports of special committees
6. Special orders
7. Unfinished business and general orders
8. New business
9. Announcements
10. Adjournment

How the Chair Handles the Order of Business

1. **Call to order**. With one rap of the gavel the chair calls the meeting to order: "The meeting will come to order." It is the duty of the chair to call the meeting to order on time.

2. **Certification of notice.** The secretary presents the certification that the required notice has been mailed or posted. The certification may be a document signed by the secretary or it may be a certificate of mailing from the postal service.

3. **Reading and approval of the minutes.** *Robert's Rules of Order Newly Revised* begins the order of business here. "The secretary will read the minutes of the previous meeting." "Are there any corrections to the minutes?" "Are there any further corrections to the minutes?"
   If there are no corrections: "The minutes are approved as read." *If there are corrections*: "The minutes are approved as corrected."

4. **Reports of officers, boards, and standing committees.** The officers and standing committees report in the order in which they are listed in the bylaws.

   The Report of the Treasurer goes here. The financial report given by the treasurer is not adopted or approved. The Report of the Auditing Committee, *or the audit,* is adopted. "The next business in order is the financial report by the treasurer." "Are there any questions on the financial report?" "The report will be filed."
   "The next business in order is reports of standing committees. Miss Jackson will report for the ... committee."

5. **Reports of special committees.** Only those scheduled to report should be called upon. "The special committee on ... will report.—Mr. Alba."

6. **Special orders.**
Any items of business that the documents specify for a particular meeting are special orders. For example, elections are usually conducted at the annual meeting. Other special orders are those motions that were postponed to a certain meeting and made special orders by a two-thirds vote.[1] "At the (date) meeting the motion '...' was made a special order for this meeting. The chair recognizes Mr. Daniels."

7. **Unfinished business and General orders.**
A motion which was pending when the meeting adjourned is taken up as unfinished business at the next meeting. "When the previous meeting was adjourned, a motion to ... was pending. The question now is on the motion to .... Is there any discussion?" General orders are those motions that were postponed to a certain meeting and general orders not reached at the previous meeting.[1] "At the September meeting consideration of ... was postponed to this meeting. Is there any discussion?" Amendments to documents are also general orders.

8. **New business**. "Is there any new business?" Members may introduce new business by making motions.

9. **Announcements.** "Are there any announcements?"

10. **Adjournment.** "If there is no objection and no further business, the meeting will be adjourned." "Since there is no objection and no further business, the meeting is adjourned." *or* "The chair declares the meeting adjourned."

Items may be added to the agenda in the appropriate places. The order of business is a generic agenda. If the meeting is large or complex, the agenda will have additional items, sometimes in great detail. All items of business will come up under a class of business on the generic agenda.

An inexperienced presiding officer will find that a script agenda is helpful. For each item of business, the words used to introduce it and dispose of it are written in at particular places on the agenda.

A copy of the agenda should be given to the secretary and the parliamentarian. This will expedite their work during the meeting.

Where notice is specified by statute, the agenda may be a required part of the notice.

[1] Motions may not be postponed beyond the next regular meeting. Even then, they may not be postponed beyond a quarterly time period.

Example

Association Agenda for a membership meeting

Call to order
Certification of notice
Report of the registration committee
- Number of proxies represented
- Number present in person

Adoption of the rules for debate
Approval of the minutes of the previous meeting
- This may be a report of the approval of the minutes by the board, or a report of a committee appointed to approve the minutes.

Appointment of committees
- Election committee

Reports of officers
- President
- Vice President
- Secretary
- Treasurer

Report of the Board of Directors
Reports of standing committees
- Landscaping committee
- Recreation committee
- Greens committee
- Maintenance committee
- Newsletter committee
- Budget committee

Reports of special committees
- Legislative liaison

Election of directors
Amendment of bylaws
- Amendment 1
- Amendment 2

New business
Announcements
Adjournment

Voting Results

Voting Results

Majority vote = more than half the votes cast, even when the result is a fraction. For example, a majority of 9 is 5, the 5 as a result of a fraction. Any uneven number of votes cast will result in a fraction of a vote in a majority vote. The count is of votes, not people.

Extraordinary majority = more than a majority. The term *extraordinary majority* should not be used unless the documents define it.

Majority plus one. Find the majority as defined above and add one. For example, 9-5 as above, 6 is a majority plus one.

Plurality vote = the largest number of votes cast.

Example, *plurality*
Mrs. C received 14 votes
Mr. A received 12 votes
Illegal votes, 7
Mrs. C is elected, because she received more votes than Mr. A, and more votes than the illegal votes.

Example, *majority*
Mrs. C received 14 votes
Mr. A received 12 votes
Illegal votes, 7
There is no majority because there were 33 votes cast, a majority of which is 17 (more than half of the votes cast). The vote must be retaken as many times as necessary for a candidate to achieve a majority.

Two-thirds vote = at least two thirds of the votes cast. Usually the vote should be counted. *See chart p. 97.*

Unanimous vote = no dissenting votes.

Tie vote = the same number of affirmative and negative votes.

Unanimous consent = no objection. This is also called general consent.

Ballot vote = usually a paper ballot where the member writes in his choice or choices. This is usually a secret ballot. A ballot vote may be used on motions as well as on elections.

Voice vote = ayes and noes.

Rising vote = alternated voting where those voting in the affirmative rise, then those voting in the negative rise. This vote is not always counted. The rising vote is taken when a member calls "Division." or "I call for a division of the assembly." A rising vote is taken when the vote is a two-thirds vote, unless another voting method, such as balloting, is used.

Counted vote = a vote that is counted because the documents require it, the chair decides to count the vote, or when a motion has been adopted to count the vote.

Voting by the chair

The chair, if a member, may vote when his vote will affect the result: to break a tie, to create a tie, to prevent a two-thirds, to create a two-thirds. The president always votes when the vote is by ballot, but may not vote again to alter the result. In any case, the president has one vote. A non-member serving as presiding officer does not have a vote at all, unless the association has given that power.

Proxy voting

General proxy = the agent may vote as he pleases on the proposal at hand.

Limited proxy = the agent is legally bound to cast the vote as marked on the limited proxy.

Non-members as directors

Non-members serving as directors vote on the proposals before the board when the documents specify that they have a vote.

Minutes

Minutes

Minutes may be used in a court of law to determine the legality of action taken by the board or assembly. Accuracy cannot be over-emphasized. It is imperative that the minutes be taken by a person who is capable of attending to details, and that members examine the minutes for accuracy.

Content of minutes

The minutes should include the following:

- Day and time of the meeting.
- The name of the association, assembly, or board, and the place of the meeting if not always the same.
- The kind of meeting: regular, special, adjourned regular, adjourned special, annual, adjourned annual, or executive session.

  Note: In some states, statutes prohibit condominium boards from meeting in executive session and voting by secret ballot.
- Who called the meeting to order and who presided. This includes any temporary presiding officer, such as a vice president or a professional parliamentarian.
- The fact of the presence of the recording secretary or a secretary *pro tempore* in the absence of the regular secretary.
- The fact of a quorum present. Some associations and boards list the names of those present and those absent. The credentials, or attendance, report is

appended to the minutes. This includes the list of voting interests present in person and by proxy.

- The fact of the approval of the minutes as written or as corrected.

- Appointments made during the meeting, such as the election committee, tellers, registrars. This includes appointments of committees to report at a future time.

- All main motions, and how they were disposed of, all points of order and appeals, and any other motions required by the association's rules to be included, except any that were withdrawn. Motions and resolutions are recorded precisely as they were adopted.

- All secondary motions that were not defeated or withdrawn, when they are necessary for the clarity of the minutes.

- Notices of motions to be made at the next meeting should be recorded in the minutes. The text of the motion for which notice was given should be recorded. When the notice is for the motion to rescind a very long motion or resolution, the title, subject, and date of adoption may be recorded instead of the complete text.

- If the association's rules demand it, the number of votes in the affirmative and negative on a matter is recorded. All counted votes are recorded. Roll call votes are entered in the minutes in full. If a member does not respond to the roll call, if it is known he is present, "present" may be entered beside his name when it is necessary to establish that there was a quorum when the vote was taken.

- Abstentions from voting may be recorded when the abstention has to do with a conflict of interest, or when the member has a *legitimate reason* for requesting that the abstention be recorded.

  Usually condominium directors are required to vote and may not abstain on principle. In this case, the abstention must be because of a conflict of interest.

- The time of adjournment is recorded as well as how the meeting was adjourned, that is, by motion or unanimous consent.

Parliamentary minutes

Parliamentary minutes include the above items plus any additional items required by the association's rules.

Literal minutes

Literal minutes are verbatim minutes. They are usually recorded by a stenographer or court reporter. All discussion is recorded as well as all subsidiary motions, the makers of the motions, the seconders, and all other motions whether adopted or not.

Signing of the minutes

The secretary signs the minutes. Even when the minutes are recorded by an employed stenographer, the secretary of the association must sign them if he was present. The secretary is not relieved of any responsibility for the accuracy of the minutes because someone else recorded them.

Corrections

Minutes are not automatically corrected when a member responds to the request by the chair for corrections to the minutes.

The secretary should check all such corrections to be certain that they are actually corrections. The secretary, or any member, may challenge a correction. When there is a dispute, a vote is taken on the correction.

Errors in motions are not corrections to the minutes. When a motion was made incorrectly and was adopted, and at a later meeting the maker of the motion makes a correction to the motion, that is not a correction to the minutes. The minutes are an accurate record of the proceedings and will record the motion as it was adopted.

The correction to a motion is accomplished by the motion *to amend something previously adopted.* This motion is recorded in the current meeting minutes. Errors in reports that are included in the minutes are treated the same way. Corrections should not be a change of history.

Minutes book

The minutes should be bound into a corporate minutes book available from office supply stores. The book will have numbered pages and a binding that may be locked when the book is full. This will prevent pages from being removed or replaced. Because of the numbered pages, any such removal will be revealed.

Elections

The complete report of the election committee should be recorded in the minutes. Occasionally associations do not wish to record the number of votes the candidates received because it might embarrass someone. That is not a valid reason to omit the tellers' report. It is important that the election be recorded accurately in case of later complications.

Amendments of documents

The complete text of any amendments to bylaws, covenants, articles of incorporation, or any other documents should be recorded completely and accurately in the minutes.

Attachments

When the minutes record that certain documents are "attached" to the minutes, they must be bound with the minutes in the permanent minute book. It is always better to write any important information directly into the minutes for approval. If there are "attachments," notations must be made on each one as to the disposition of the paper, such as "adopted," "approved," or "heard for information," etc. The minutes will record how each was disposed of. These notations must be signed by the secretary.

Resolutions and motions

Resolutions and motions should be recorded in the minutes exactly as they were adopted. Important motions and resolutions should be required to be in writing. These written motions may be bound into the minutes book or bound into a separate book.

All such documents should be dated and notations made on them of their disposition in the meeting. When these documents are bound into the minute book, the secretary should keep a separate typewritten record of them.

Motions and resolutions remain in effect as adopted until they are amended or rescinded. Many such motions establish standing rules that affect the way the association does business. This record should be readily available for research.

Reading and approval of the minutes

The reading of the minutes may be dispensed with when the minutes have been distributed prior to the meeting at which they will be approved. However, the *correction and approval* of the minutes should not be dispensed with. If the condominium is required to post the minutes, the *approved* minutes are posted.

Minutes of an executive session should be read and approved in executive session.

Minutes are the accurate history of the association's adopted business, and should only include those items of legal interest to the association. If further records of events are desired, a historian or other person may be appointed to keep a separate record.

Committees

Committees

Committee: One or more persons, elected or appointed, to consider or investigate certain matters. 1. *Standing Committees* have a continuing existence, and 2. *Special Committees* are temporary and go out of existence when they have fulfilled their instructions and have made a final report.

- Standing committee members may serve the same term as the officers.

- If the bylaws provide for certain standing committees, there can be no others unless the bylaws provide for other means of establishing them.

- A committee appointed "with power" has the power to act on behalf of the association only as specifically authorized.

- If the bylaws do not specify the method of electing or appointing committees, the method can be decided by general consent or by a majority vote at the time the committee is established.

- The power to appoint committees carries with it the power to appoint the chairmen and to fill vacancies in the committees.

- The bylaws or the assembly may give the president the power to appoint committees.

- The president is *ex officio* a member of committees when specified in the bylaws.

- The president, *ex officio,* is not counted in the quorum, but may participate in debate, make motions and vote.

- A quorum of a committee is a majority of its members.

- Sub-committees report to the committee, not to the assembly.

- The first named person to a committee serves as chairman unless the bylaws specify the method of choosing committee chairmen.

- The committee chairman may participate in debate, make motions and vote.

- Motions to limit debate are not allowed in committee.

- No second is required to a committee recommendation or motion unless it is from a committee of one.

- An entire committee report is not usually adopted.

- To *receive* a committee report merely means to hear it, nothing more.

- Ad hoc. Committees *ad hoc* are special committees, as are such groups as task groups, task forces, etc. Regardless of what they are called, committees are standing committees and special committees.

Committee Reports

- All reports are presented in the third person singular. For example: "the president (or your president) reports," "the committee reports," "the secretary reports."

- The reporting member of the committee, usually the chairman, reads the report and moves the adoption of any recommendations contained in the report.

- Committee reports consist of: name, the facts found, recommendations, and signatures.

- A written report is signed by all committee members who concur, with the chairman's signing first, or, if signed only by the chairman, he writes *Chairman* after his name.

- "Respectfully submitted" is no longer used.

An association that has a very small board will find it very helpful to appoint non-board members to committees. This helps to make the board more efficient by including others to help do the work of the association. It also increases the confidence of the owners that the board is interested in the opinion and experience of the community members on important matters.

Annual Meetings
Membership (Owners') Meetings

Annual Meetings
Membership (Owners') Meetings

Membership, or owners', meetings are meetings of the corporation as well as of the association.

Notice

The annual meeting requires careful planning. The notices of meetings and elections must be posted or mailed on time. The notice will include amendments to the documents and proxies for the unit owners to fill in and send to the designated proxy agent.

The package containing the notice will include explanations for the enclosed papers. The notice will include a time limit for returning proxies and ballots.

Meeting committees

The board of directors will appoint an election committee for the election of officers and a tellers' committee to count the votes of the voting interests during the meeting. In a small association, these two committees may be combined.

A registration or credentials committee will be appointed to check the voters as they arrive to be sure that all who will be voting are members, and that anyone carrying proxies has registered them.

Registration of proxies

Proxies must be registered before the meeting. The registration will include the proxy owner and his agent. An owner may revoke his proxy at any time before the meeting. For example, he may choose to go to the meeting and cast his vote in person. There is always the possibility that he will have changed his preference for an agent.

Proxies may be sent directly to the secretary of the association for use by the board.

The votes marked on the limited proxies will be used by the election, or tellers', committee.

General proxies need only be counted and registered in the name of the proxy signer and his agent.

Rules for debate

Rules for limiting debate are written by a rules committee or the board. These rules are usually to limit the number of times a member may speak in debate, and how long each time.

The need for rules will depend upon the size of the meeting and the personality of the membership. If there have been problems with meetings lasting too long, rules for debate can be very helpful.

Example: *Members speaking in debate shall speak no more than twice on the same question and no longer than two minutes each time.*

The rules are adopted by a two-thirds vote or by general consent.

Members attending the meeting should be handed a copy of the proposed rules upon entering the hall unless the rules were included in the notice package.

Procedure for membership meetings is formal. Following are the rules for motions used in owners' meetings, even where the number may be very small. Owners' meetings include regular, special, and annual meetings.

Motions

How to Complete Action on a Motion

1. The member rises, addresses the Chair: "Mr. (or) Madam President," and waits for recognition.

2. The Chair recognizes the member (grants him the floor).

3. The member makes a motion: "I move that...."

4. Another member seconds the motion.

5. The Chair *states* the motion and opens the floor to debate (on debatable motions). "It is moved and seconded that ... Is there any discussion?" *or* "Are you ready for the question?"

6. Members discuss the motion after being granted the floor by the Chair.

7. After debate, the Chair repeats the motion and *puts* the question (takes the vote). "The question is on the motion that .... Those in favor, say *aye*. Those opposed, say *no*. The *ayes* have it and the motion is adopted."

   Action on a motion is not complete until the Chair has announced the result of the vote.

Note: When a committee reports, the reporting member moves the adoption of any recommendations contained in the report. Committee motions and resolutions do not require a second if the committee consists of more than one person. Some state statutes require that a committee of a corporation consist of at least two members.

Following is a list of the classes of motions used in formal assemblies.

Classes of Motions

- **Main Motions** - bring business before the assembly:
  a. *An Original Main Motion* - introduces a *new* subject for consideration.
  b. *An Incidental Main Motion* - is incidental to the business of the assembly.

  An Incidental Main Motion does not bring a new subject for consideration. Some incidental main motions resemble motions of other classes, but differ in their rules and in when they may be introduced.

- **Subsidiary Motions** - assist the assembly in disposing of the main motion. The subsidiary motions are:
  to postpone indefinitely
  to amend
  to refer to a committee
  to postpone to a certain time
  to limit or extend limits of debate
  to order the previous question, and
  to lay the question on the table.

- **Privileged Motions** - are privileged because they relate to matters of special or immediate importance. The privileged motions are:
  to call for the orders of the day
  to raise a question of privilege
  to recess
  to adjourn, and
  to fix the time to which to adjourn.

- **Incidental Motions** - relate to the pending business in some way.

- **Motions That Bring A Question Again Before The Assembly**:
  Take from the table
  Amend something previously adopted
  Rescind
  Discharge a committee, and
  Reconsider

Precedence

(Rank of motions)

The main motion, the subsidiary motions, and the privileged motions have what is called *precedence.* That is, they have a rank to each other.

A motion *takes precedence over* another motion.

The lowest ranking motion in the sequence is the main motion and the highest ranking is the motion to fix the time to continue a meeting to a later date (fix the time to which to adjourn).

For example, when a main motion is pending, any motion of greater rank is in order. When a motion to refer the main motion to a committee is pending, the motions of lower rank are not in order.

Precedence tells the maker of the motion when a certain motion is in order.

The thirteen ranking motions, beginning with the highest ranking, are:

Privileged motions:

Fix the time to which to adjourn
Adjourn
Recess
Raise a question of privilege
Call for the orders of the day

Subsidiary motions:

Lay the question on the table
Previous question
Limit or extend the limits of debate
Postpone to a certain time
Refer to a committee
Amend the main motion
Postpone indefinitely

Main Motion

The rules governing the use of these motions begin on the following page.

The Main Motion

A ***Main Motion*** is a proposition that something be done or that something is the opinion of the assembly. There are two types of main motions— original main motions and incidental main motions.

An ***Original Main Motion*** brings before the assembly some new subject for consideration and action.

An ***Incidental Main Motion*** is a main motion that is incidental to the business of the assembly or to its previously taken action. See page 59 for examples of this type of motion.

A *Resolution* is a main motion and should be in writing. A very important motion should be in the form of a resolution. A resolution may or may not have a preamble. The preamble may be a brief statement of background.

Rules Relating to the Main Motion:

- It may be made when no other business is pending.
- It may not conflict with the bylaws, Articles of Incorporation, local, state or national law, or rules of a superior body. If it so conflicts and is adopted, it is invalid (null and void).
- It may not conflict with or be substantially the same as a motion previously adopted or rejected by the assembly during the same session, or a motion that has been introduced and has not been finally disposed of, or a motion that will come up under unfinished business.
- It may have applied to it any subsidiary motion, that is, it may be amended, committed, postponed, etc. It is the lowest ranking motion.

- A main motion, when possible, should be in the affirmative rather than the negative form.

- A main motion requires recognition by the chair. It requires a second, it is debatable, it requires a majority vote for adoption, and it may be reconsidered.

- A main motion is amendable.
  A main motion may be amended to the first and second degrees. The primary amendment must be germane to the main motion, and the secondary amendment must be germane to the primary amendment. An amendment of the third degree is not in order.

- A main motion should be concise, unambiguous, and contain all of the information needed to carry through on the action proposed (what, when, where, how, who). Say what you mean in as few words as possible. Motions are entered into the minutes the way the chair states them.

- To *Amend the Bylaws* is an incidental main motion that may be amended to the first and second degrees. There are special rules for amending the bylaws. This is a form of the Incidental Main Motion *To Amend Something Previously Adopted.*

Note: There may be statutes regarding use of limited proxies for voting on amendments in a meeting. Usually amendments from the floor are not allowed when the number of limited proxies is greater than the number of voting interests present in person. According to the rules of some states, amendments to motions that were in the notice may not be amended from the floor when there are limited proxies involved.

Subsidiary Motions

Subsidiary Motions apply to the main motion in different ways to modify it, delay action on it, or otherwise dispose of it.

To Postpone Indefinitely

The purpose of the motion *To Postpone Indefinitely* is to reject (or kill) the main motion for the remainder of the session. This is the lowest ranking subsidiary motion. It ranks just above the *Main Motion.* It is not in order if anything except the main motion is pending.

This motion, while pending, opens the main motion to debate; therefore, members who have exhausted their right to speak have another opportunity to debate the main motion.

> **Example:** *"I move that the question be postponed indefinitely."*

Rules:

it requires recognition
it requires a second
it is debatable
it is not amendable
it requires a majority vote to adopt, and
only an affirmative vote may be reconsidered

To Amend

The purpose of the motion to amend is to alter the wording of the main motion.

The motion *To Amend* ranks just above the motion *To Postpone Indefinitely* when applied to the main motion.

Amendments change the wording of a motion or resolution by the following three methods: To insert or to add, to strike out, and to strike out and insert.

1. a. To insert words, or to add words at the end.
   b. To insert a paragraph, or to add a paragraph.
2. a. To strike out words.
   b. To strike out a paragraph.
3. a. To strike out and insert words.
   b. To substitute (paragraphs).

An amendment must be *germane*. That is, it must relate to the motion it is proposed to amend. An amendment may also be amended, using the methods described above. However, there can be only one primary amendment and one secondary amendment pending at the same time, and there can be no amendment of the third degree.

Rules:
it requires recognition
it requires a second
it is debatable
it may be amended
it requires a majority vote for adoption, and
it may be reconsidered

When many words are to be changed in a motion, the preferred method of amendment is *To Substitute.*

Amendment by Substitution

1. Amendment by Substitution applies to a paragraph, a series of paragraphs, or to an entire resolution.

2. Amendment by substitution is a primary amendment and must be germane.

3. While the proposed substitute is pending, secondary amendments may be made to either the pending question or to the proposed substitute, but only one at a time.

4. While the substitute is pending, debate can go into the merits of both the pending question and the proposed substitute.

5. The pending question is amended first, then the proposed substitute may be amended.

6. After both the pending question and the proposed substitute are perfected by amendment, the Chair puts the question on substituting the proposed substitute for the pending question. If the amendment by substitution is adopted, the substitute becomes the *amended motion*. The original motion is no longer pending.

7. At this time, the amended motion may be further amended only by adding words at the end.

8. The Chair puts the question (takes the vote) on the amended motion.

Examples: *"I move to substitute for the pending question the following: That ...."*
"I move to substitute for paragraph three of the resolution the following: ...."

To Refer to a Committee

The purpose of this motion is to place a question in the hands of a standing or special committee. It *ranks* just above the motion *To Amend.*

Debate on the motion to commit is limited to: The appropriateness of committing the main question, instructions to the committee, and to which committee to refer the question.

Amendment is limited to: designating another committee, adding instructions, and changing the method of appointment of the committee.

Examples:

"I move to refer the pending question to a committee of three appointed by the President, and that the committee report at the next meeting."

"I move that the question be referred to the Greens Committee."

Rules:

it requires recognition
it requires a second
it is debatable as to the advisability of referring the main question to a committee
it is amendable as to which committee, how many members shall serve on it, and how the committee shall be appointed
it requires a majority vote for adoption, and
it may be reconsidered

To Postpone to a Certain Time

The purpose of this motion is to postpone action on a pending question to a definite day, meeting, or hour.

It *ranks* just above the motion *To Commit.* Postponed questions come up under Unfinished Business and General Orders unless made a general order for a certain hour (majority vote), or a Special Order (two-thirds vote).

Debate is limited to the merits of postponement and the suitability of the time.

Amendment is limited as to time, and as to making a special order. *A question cannot be postponed beyond the next regular meeting.* To take up a postponed question before the specified time requires a suspension of the rules (two-thirds vote).

Examples:

"I move to postpone consideration of the motion until the next meeting."

"I move to postpone consideration of the question until 3:00 P.M.."

Rules:

it requires recognition
it requires a second
it is debatable
it may be amended
it requires a majority vote for adoption, and
it may be reconsidered

To Modify Debate

The purpose of this motion is to *limit or extend the limits* of debate as to time, length of speeches, or number of speeches members may make. It *ranks* just above the motion *To Postpone to a Certain Time.* This motion requires a two-thirds vote to carry.

The motion *To Modify Debate* is *not debatable* and may only be *amended* as to time and number and length of speeches.

Amendment of the motion requires only a majority vote, but adoption of the motion requires a two-thirds vote.

To Modify Debate applies only to the immediately pending question, and others as specified in the motion.

Examples:
"I move that debate on the question be closed and that the vote be taken at 1:00 P.M."
"I move that debate on the pending question be limited to 12 minutes."
"I move that in debate on the pending question, members be allowed to speak only once and no longer than 5 minutes."

Rules:

it requires recognition
it requires a second
it is not debatable
it is amendable
it requires a two-thirds vote for adoption, and
it may be reconsidered

The Previous Question

The purpose of this motion is to close debate, to prevent further amendment, and to proceed immediately to the vote. It *ranks* just above the motion *To Modify Debate.*

This motion requires a two-thirds vote for adoption. *"I move the previous question."*

A call from a member, "Question! Question!" or "I call the question!" does not automatically close debate. Debate is a right of members and cannot be denied by the demand of a single member.

The Previous Question may be called on a motion that is not debatable but is amendable. Adoption of the motion in that case prevents amendment. The motion for the Previous Question is *not debatable.*

The Previous Question is exhausted at the adjournment of the session in which it was adopted.
"Exhausted" means that any unexecuted part of the motion is no longer in effect after a specific time.

This motion, if adopted, stops debate on the immediately pending question. If it is desired to stop debate on a main motion with adhering motions such as amendments, the form is: *"I move the previous question on all pending motions."*

Rules:

it requires recognition
it requires a second
it is not debatable
it is not amendable
it requires a two-thirds vote to adopt, and
it may be reconsidered

To Lay the Question on the Table

The purpose of this motion is to lay aside a question *temporarily* to take up a matter of urgent business.

This is the *highest ranking* of the subsidiary motions. *This motion is not debatable and cannot be qualified in any way.* It may not be amended.

This is a frequently misused motion. If the intent of the maker of the motion is to kill the motion under discussion, *To Lay The Question on The Table* is not in order, and should not be allowed by the Chair.

"I move that the question be laid on the table."

A motion laid on the table must be taken from the table by a motion of any member before the adjournment of the next regular meeting or the question dies.

See: To take from the table, page 52.

Rules:

it requires recognition
it is not debatable
it is not amendable
it requires a majority vote to adopt, and
it may not be reconsidered

Privileged Motions

Privileged motions are of such importance that they take precedence over all other motions. Privileged motions are not debatable.

To Call For the Orders of the Day

This is the lowest ranking of the five Privileged motions. It is used to demand that an item in the order of business be taken up. It is used when there is an obvious and unnecessary deviation from the adopted order of business or agenda. *"I call for the orders of the day."*

Rules:

it does not require a second because it is a demand by a single member
it is not debatable
it is not amendable
it requires no vote unless there is an objection.
A two-thirds vote in the negative is required to refuse to proceed to the orders of the day.

To Raise a Question of Privilege

This is a motion relating to the safety or comfort of the *assembly*, e.g., to open a window, reduce noise, etc. *"Mr. President, I rise to a question of privilege." Raising a question is privileged.* The question of privilege raised does not have the same consideration. The chair rules on the admissibility of the question.

Rules:

it requires recognition
it does not require a second
it is not debatable
it is not amendable, and
it may not be reconsidered

To Take a Recess

This provides a break in a meeting, usually for a few minutes, but it can be for longer. Examples: *"I move that we recess for 15 minutes."* *"I move that we recess until 1:00 P.M."*

Rules:

it requires recognition
it requires a second
it is not debatable
it may be amended, and
it requires a majority vote to adopt

To Adjourn

This motion, if adopted, officially closes the meeting. As a privileged motion, it cannot be qualified in any way. The *Chair* must declare the meeting adjourned. There are motions that can be made after the motion to adjourn is adopted and before the Chair declares the meeting adjourned.
"Madam President, I move to adjourn."

Rules:

it requires recognition
it requires a second
it is not debatable
it is not amendable, and
it requires a majority vote to adopt

If the motion is adopted, the meeting is closed when the chair declares the meeting adjourned. When there is no motion to adjourn, the Chair may adjourn a meeting by general consent.

Steps that may be taken while the motion to adjourn is pending and before the Chair has declared the meeting adjourned: announcements, notices of motions to be made at the next meeting, business *requiring* attention, to *make* the motion to *reconsider*, but not to *take up* reconsideration, and to *fix the time to which to adjourn.*

To Fix the Time To Which to Adjourn

This is the highest ranking of the privileged motions and of the 13 ranking motions. This motion designates another day or time to which to continue the present meeting.

> **Example:** *"I move that when we adjourn, we adjourn to meet tomorrow at 3:00 P.M."*

If adopted, this means that the present meeting will continue tomorrow at three o'clock. This motion does not adjourn a meeting. The minutes will reflect that the adjourned meeting is a continuation of the present meeting.

Rules:

it requires a second
it is not debatable
it is amendable as to the date and time, and
it requires a majority vote to adopt

When a proxy states that it is valid for the designated meeting and any continuation thereof, this motion provides for such a continued meeting when necessary.

Motions That Bring a Question Again Before the Assembly

(Bring Back Motions)

To Reconsider

The motion to *Reconsider the Vote* must be made by a member who voted on the prevailing side, affirmative *or* negative. It is debatable if the motion to be reconsidered is debatable.

To *make* the motion to reconsider takes precedence of all other motions. *Consideration* of a motion has the same *rank* as the motion to be reconsidered.

Reconsideration may be moved only on the same day as the vote on the motion to be reconsidered was taken, or in a session of more than one day–the same day or the next *business* day.

This motion may be *made* after the motion to adjourn has been adopted, but the chair has not yet declared the meeting adjourned, although the question to be reconsidered may not be *taken up* at that time.

Reconsideration, when adopted, opens the main question to debate again, before the vote is retaken.

"I move to reconsider the vote on the motion that ...."

Rules:

it requires recognition
it requires a second
it is debatable if the motion to be reconsidered is debatable
it may not be amended
it requires a majority vote to adopt, and
it may not be reconsidered

To Take From the Table

This motion is to take from the table a motion that was laid on the table. Any member may make the motion. *"I move to take from the table the motion that ...."*

When a question is taken from the table, debate resumes where it left off when it was laid on the table.

Rules:

it requires recognition
it requires a second
it is not debatable
it is not amendable
it requires a majority vote to adopt, and
it may not be reconsidered

To Rescind

This is *an Incidental Main Motion.* The motion to Rescind is used to repeal an action that the assembly has taken previously. A motion cannot be rescinded after action has been taken, such as the signing of a contract, a resignation, etc. This motion requires a two-thirds vote, or a majority of the entire membership, or a majority vote with previous notice. *"I move to rescind the motion that ...."*

Rules:

it requires recognition
it requires a second
it is debatable
it may be amended, and
it requires a majority vote with notice,
a two-thirds vote without notice, or a majority
of the entire membership

To Discharge a Committee

The assembly takes a matter out of the hands of a committee before the committee has made a final report. The assembly considers the subject that had been referred to the committee. *"I move to discharge the committee to which was referred the motion that ... and take up the question."*

Rules:

it may be made only when no other motion is pending
it requires recognition
it requires a second
it is debatable
it is amendable, and
it requires a majority vote with notice or a two-thirds vote without notice to adopt
Only the negative vote may be reconsidered.

To Amend Something Previously Adopted

This motion can be applied to main motions, bylaws, special rules of order, and minutes of previous meetings.

The vote required for adoption is the same as *To Rescind*, except in the case of amendment of the bylaws, which is two-thirds *and* previous notice unless the bylaws or other documents specify otherwise. *"I move to amend the previously adopted motion that ... by striking out the words ... and inserting the words ...."*

Rules:

it may be made when no other motion is pending
it requires recognition
it requires a second
it is debatable
it is amendable, and
it requires a majority vote with notice or a two-thirds vote without notice to adopt

Incidental Motions

This class of motions deals with procedures arising out of: other pending motions, another motion or item of business. These motions are incidental to the business that is pending or that has been pending or will be pending. *Incidental Motions* are voted on as they arise, and most are not debatable.

Some Incidental Motions:

Method of Voting

"I move that the vote on the motion ... be taken by ballot." *"I move that voting in the election be by ballot."* (This motion may be made when the bylaws do not specify the method of voting.)

Rules:

it requires recognition
it requires a second
it is not debatable
it is amendable, and
it requires a majority vote for adoption

Division of the Question

The purpose of this motion is to divide a question that has more than one part, each part capable of standing alone as a separate motion. *"I move to divide the question."*

Rules:

it requires recognition
it requires a second
it is not debatable
it is amendable, and
it requires a majority vote to adopt

Division of the Assembly

This is a call for a *rising* vote. *"I doubt the vote." "I question the vote." "I call for a division."*

A rising vote may be demanded by a single member, without a second. The purpose is to verify a voice vote that appears to be close.

Rules:

it does not require a second because it is a demand
it is not debatable
it is not amendable
it is out of order when the result of the vote is very clear

On important or controversial questions the Chair, on his own initiative, may take a *counted rising vote.* If the chair is unsure of the vote, a rising vote will help to verify the result.

For example, when the voices are louder on the aye or no, they may seem to be in the majority. The chair should take the responsibility to ensure that there is no doubt of the correct result.

A member may make the motion to have the vote counted. *"I move that the vote be counted."*

Although the motion *division of the assembly* is a demand, the motion *to count the vote* is not. The motion *to count the vote* is an incidental motion. It requires a second and a majority vote to carry.

Withdraw a Motion

Before a motion is stated by the Chair as pending, the maker of the motion may withdraw his motion without permission of the assembly or the seconder.

After the question has been stated by the Chair, it is in the possession of the assembly. The maker of the motion must request that the motion be withdrawn.

> **Example:** *"I request permission to withdraw the motion."*

Rules:

The Chair will usually withdraw a motion by general consent.

If there is an objection to withdrawal, a vote must be taken on whether to permit withdrawal of the motion. In that case a majority vote will withdraw the motion.

When the motion to withdraw a motion is made by another member after the request has been made by the maker, no second is required.

Point of Order

This motion should be used when there is a violation of the rules of order, bylaws, or laws of the land.

> **Example:** *"Mr. President, I rise to a point of order."* Chair: *"State your point of order."* The member raises his point, referring to the parliamentary authority, bylaws or other rules. The chair will either say *"Your point is well taken."* and correct the procedure, or *"Your point is not well taken."* and explain why.

No other members may debate the point unless the Chair asks for information from the parliamentarian or other knowledgeable member, or the chair submits the question to the assembly for a decision.

The motion is out of order if it is used to delay the meeting or to cause disruption. It should apply to serious infractions of the rules, it should not be used frivolously. A member who constantly raises points of order on minor points is a nuisance.

Rules:

no second is required
it is not debatable
it is not amendable, and
the chair rules
If the chair rules the point not well taken, one member and a seconder may appeal from the decision of the chair.

Appeal

After a point of order has been not well taken, and the member still believes that the chair is incorrect, the member and a seconder may appeal.

The assembly rules on whether to sustain the decision of the chair.

> "I appeal from the decision of the chair."

Rules:

it is limited to rulings by the chair
it requires recognition
it requires a second
it is debatable if the question on which the appeal was made is debatable, and not debatable if it relates to indecorum or rules of speaking, or to the priority of business
it is not amendable
a majority or a tie vote sustains the chair, and the chair may vote to create the tie, and
it may be reconsidered

Parliamentary Inquiry

A member rises to ask a question on parliamentary procedure relating to the business of the assembly.

> **Example:** *"I rise to a parliamentary inquiry." "Madam President, would it be in order at this time to ...." or "Mr. Chairman, what vote is required to adopt the pending motion? "*

Rules:

it does not require a second because it is a request
it is not debatable
it is not amendable, and
the chair answers the question

Point of Information

A member rises to ask a question relating to the business of the assembly or a pending motion. *"Mr. President, I rise for information."* The Chair will say, *"State your question."* and the member asks his question.

The question is directed to the Chair or to another member *through* the Chair, not directly from one member to another.

Rules:

it does not require a second because it is a request
it is not debatable
it is not amendable, and
the chair answers the question or directs the question to another knowledgeable member

NOTE: Incidental motions should not be confused with *Incidental main motions.* Incidental main motions are a separate class of motions.

Incidental Main Motions

Incidental Main Motions relate to the business of the assembly and do not introduce a new subject for consideration.

Incidental Main Motions resemble motions of other classes, but may only be made when no other business is pending.

Incidental Main Motions which require a majority vote for adoption

Adjourn, when ***qualified,*** such as, *"I move that we adjourn at five o'clock."* or when no provision has been made for another meeting (such as a continuation annual meeting when needed to finish business required by the bylaws).

Adopt a committee recommendation not related to a referred motion. When a committee chairman has reported committee recommendations, but has not moved to adopt them, any member may do so.

Rules:

it requires a second
it is amendable
it is debatable, and
it requires a majority vote to adopt

Fix the Time to Which to Adjourn, when no other business is pending. Otherwise this is a privileged motion.

Rules:

it requires a second
it is debatable
it is amendable, and
it requires a majority vote to adopt

Prescribe the Method of Nominations, when no election is pending. *"I move that in the election tomorrow morning, we nominate by ballot."*

Rules:

it requires a second
it is debatable
it is amendable, and
it requires a majority vote to adopt

Ratify emergency action taken at a meeting where there was no quorum. *"I move to ratify the action of the president taken during the emergency meeting on May 12, that the leaking roof be repaired at a cost of ...."*

Rules:

it requires a second
it is debatable
it is amendable, and
it requires a majority vote to adopt

Recess, when no other business is pending. *"I move that we take a recess at 5:00."*

Rules:

it requires a second
it is debatable
it is amendable, and
it requires a majority vote to adopt

Suspend a standing rule for the duration of the session.

Rules:

it requires a second, and
it requires a majority vote to adopt

Incidental Main Motions which require a two-thirds vote for adoption

Limit Debate or limit the number of times a member may speak on a question, when no question is pending.

Rules:

it requires a second
it is not debatable
it is amendable, and
it requires a two-thirds vote for adoption

Incidental Main Motions which require for adoption a vote of: majority with notice, or two-thirds, or a majority of the entire membership

Amend Something Previously Adopted
Postpone an *event* or action previously adopted.
Rescind a previously adopted action.

Rules:

These motions require a second
they are debatable
they are amendable, and
they require a two-thirds vote for adoption.

Incidental Main Motion which requires previous notice and two-thirds vote for adoption:

Amend the Bylaws. This is a form of the motion to amend something previously adopted. However, amendment of bylaws has special rules.

Note: Motions to amend. When notice has been given of motion to amend a document, or to make assessments, no greater change than that given in the notice may be made. For example, if an amount has been given in the notice, an amendment is not in order for a lesser amount than in the existing rule nor a greater amount than was proposed in the notice.

Amendments to association documents should be written by the association attorney or at least checked by the attorney before notice is sent. This will assure that the amendments will conform with all relevant statutes.

The motion *objection to the consideration of the question* cannot be applied to an Incidental Main Motion.

It is important to remember that Incidental Main Motions that resemble other classes of motions *are in order only when no other motions are pending.*

As main motions, they require a second, are debatable, amendable, and with the exceptions noted above, require a majority vote for adoption.

MOTION	S	D	A	V	R
RANK **Privileged Motions**					
Fix the time to which to adjourn	Yes	No	Yes	Maj.	No
Adjourn	Yes	No	No	Maj.	No
Recess	Yes	No	Yes	Maj.	No
Raise a question of privilege	No	No	No	CR	No
Call for the orders of the day	No	No	No	Demand	No
RANK **Subsidiary Motions**					
Lay the question on the table	Yes	No	No	Maj.	No
Previous question	Yes	No	No	2/3	Yes
Modify limits of debate	Yes	No	Yes	2/3	Yes
Postpone to a certain time	Yes	Yes	Yes	Maj.	Yes
Refer to a committee	Yes	Yes	Yes	Maj.	Yes
Amend the main motion	Yes	Yes	Yes	Maj.	Yes
Postpone indefinitely	Yes	Yes	No	Maj.	Aff. only
RANK **Main Motion**					
Main Motion	Yes	Yes	Yes	Maj.	Yes
Motions That Bring a Question Again Before the Assembly					
Take from the table	Yes	No	No	Maj.	No
Rescind Amend something previously adopted Discharge a committee	Yes	Yes	Yes	**	N. only
Reconsider	Yes	***	No	Maj.	No

** majority with notice or 2/3
*** yes, if question to be reconsidered is
Aff.= affirmative Maj. = majority CR = chair rules

N.= negative S = second A = amend D = debate V = vote R = reconsider

Incidental Motions	S	D	A	V	R
Appeal from the decision of the chair	Yes	*No	N.	Maj.	Yes
Be excused from a duty	No	Yes	Yes	Maj.	N. only
Call for a separate vote	No	No	No	Demand	No
Close nominations	Yes	No	Yes	2/3	No
Close the polls	Yes	No	Yes	2/3	No
Consider seriatim	Yes	No	Yes	Maj.	No
Count the vote	Yes	No	Yes	Maj.	No
Create a blank	Yes	No	Yes	Maj.	No
Divide the assembly	No	No	No	Demand	No
Divide the question	Yes	No	Yes	Maj.	No
Method of voting	Yes	No	Yes	Maj.	Yes
Point of order	No	No	No	**	No
Point of information	No	No	No	NV	No
Reopen nominations	Yes	No	Yes	Maj.	N. only
Reopen the polls	Yes	No	Yes	Maj.	N. only
Request to withdraw a motion	No	No	No	Maj.	N. only
Suspend rules of order	Yes	No	No	2/3	No
Suspend standing rules	Yes	No	No	Maj.	No
Vote by ballot	Yes	No	Yes	Maj.	Yes

* depends on ruling appealed
** chair rules NV = no vote Maj. = majority N = negative

S = second A = amend D = debate V = vote R = reconsider

Duties of Officers

Duties of Officers

President

As the presiding officer of the assembly, the duties are:

1. To call the meeting to order on time.

2. To announce the business to come before the assembly, following the order of business or agenda adopted by the assembly.

3. To recognize members who are entitled to the floor for discussion, questions, or to bring business before the assembly.

4. To state the questions brought before the assembly, to put the vote on all questions not decided by general consent, and to announce the result of the vote. Action is not complete on any business until the Chair has declared the result of the vote.

5. To maintain order, to rule on matters of parliamentary procedure, and to do so impartially.

6. To expedite business without abusing the power of the office.

7. To be thoroughly familiar with all rules and documents of the association — bylaws, rules of order, standing rules, and others.

8. To have on hand for quick reference: bylaws, standing rules, special rules of order, parliamentary authority, lists of committees, and agenda.

The Chair never debates a question from the chair. He relinquishes the chair to a vice president when he debates and remains out of the chair until the question has been resolved. An exception to this is in a small-board meeting.

The president appoints committees as specified in the bylaws and is a member *ex officio* of committees only when the bylaws provide.

Vice President

The vice presidents serve instead of the president in the absence of the president. The vice presidents serve in this capacity in the order in which they are listed in the bylaws.

The vice president automatically fills the office of president in the event of a vacancy in that office unless the bylaws provide otherwise. The bylaws may specify other duties for the vice presidents.

Secretary

The secretary is the recording officer of the association, and is the custodian of the records. The secretary keeps accurate minutes of all meetings, and signs the minutes and other documents as required.

The minutes are the responsibility of the secretary even when taken and transcribed by a staff member. The minutes are signed by the secretary, who is responsible for their accuracy.

Treasurer

The Treasurer is entrusted with custody of the funds of the association, keeps thorough and accurate financial records as required, and makes regular reports of disbursements and income. The treasurer disburses funds only as authorized, making a financial report to the membership annually, and submitting the financial records for audit as specified in the bylaws and as ordered by the board or the membership. Other duties may be specified by the bylaws.

Parliamentarian

The parliamentarian should be knowledgeable in parliamentary procedure for all situations in which the meeting may find itself.

The parliamentarian never rules on a question. That is the duty of the Chair.

The parliamentarian speaks to the assembly only when requested and that should be seldom. The presiding officer and the parliamentarian should agree in advance on the way in which the Chair will be advised during meetings so that the consulting will be as inconspicuous as possible.

The presiding officer must be impartial and always appear to be impartial. That can be impossible if the parliamentarian is not impartial also.

If your association wishes to allow the *member* parliamentarian to vote and to speak in debate, adopt a special rule of order that allows it.

The presiding officer may take the advice of the parliamentarian or not. The Chair rules. The parliamentarian only advises.

A *professional* parliamentarian, who is not a member of the association, should be retained for meetings such as annual meetings and when there are many conflicts among members. A registered parliamentarian will be able to advise the association on its rules.

The professional parliamentarian will require a copy of the bylaws and other rules in sufficient time to become familiar with them. The parliamentarian will require a copy of the minutes of the previous meeting. The parliamentarian should attend board meetings before the annual meeting begins.

Boards of Directors Meetings

How to conduct a board meeting

Boards of Directors Meetings

How to conduct a board meeting

Small boards

Small boards use a much less formal procedure than large assemblies such as owners' meetings. The procedure differs in the following aspects:

Business is transacted in large boards according to the same rules as more formal assemblies such as an owners' meeting. In smaller boards, the formal rules apply except for a few instances where too much formality would stifle progress.

Association boards must take care that all motions are properly adopted and recorded.

Association boards are usually small, under twelve. In a small board meeting:

- Members are not required to obtain the floor before making motions or speaking, nor to rise when addressing the chair.
- Motions need not be seconded.
- There is no limit to the number of times a member can speak to a question, and motions to close or limit debate generally should not be entertained.
- Informal discussion of a subject is permitted while no motion is pending.
- The chairman can speak in discussion without relinquishing the chair, and he usually can make motions and vote on all questions.

Some statutes require that all association board members vote. In that case, the votes are recorded in the minutes by name.

Notice

Proper notice of meetings must be sent to all directors. In some cases, notice must be posted to inform owners of agenda items.

Call to order

The chair calls the meeting to order at the appointed time. Preliminary remarks from the chair about the day's agenda are in order, as well as any instructions for staff or consultants who are in attendance. The chair reads the agenda and proceeds to the first item of business.

Certification of notice

Usually, the first item on the agenda is the certification by the secretary that proper notice has been given. In small associations, a written certification signed by the secretary is usually sufficient. In larger associations, and especially when the notice contained proposals for assessments, a certification of mailing from the post office should be filed along with the secretary's signature.

When notices have been sent by certified mail, the certificate of mailing is sufficient.

Reading and approval of the minutes.

The next business in order is the reading and approval of the minutes of the previous meeting.

If the directors have received the minutes of the previous meeting along with the notice of meeting, reading them usually is not necessary unless a director asks for them to be read.

When the board of directors meeting is open to unit owners, the minutes should be read.

The minutes may be approved by general consent. That means that there is no vote on approval, but no director objects. The chair says, "Are there any corrections to the minutes?" If there are no corrections, the chair says, "The minutes are approved as read, (or as distributed)." If there are corrections, the chair says, "The minutes are approved as corrected." If a motion to approve the minutes is made, a majority vote is required.

When minutes are published, the corrected minutes should be used, so that there will be no misunderstanding as to the exact business that was conducted.

If state statutes require that minutes must be filed with the state, only corrected minutes are sent.

Directors must read the minutes very carefully for accuracy. Minutes are the official record of business transacted and may be used in a court of law as evidence.

A correction to the minutes is debatable. If directors do not agree on the correction, a vote is taken. A majority vote is sufficient to make the correction.

In some states, posting of the minutes is required. When this is a rule, the corrected minutes are posted. When uncorrected minutes have been posted and corrections have been made, it is a good procedure to post both the uncorrected copy and the corrected copy, with the older document marked to show the corrections.

Quorum

A quorum for a board of directors meeting is a majority of the number of directors prescribed by the association documents. The bylaws may prescribe a lower number, but not usually less than one-third of the prescribed number of directors. This means that when there is a vacancy on the board, the quorum remains at the same number as before the vacancy. The solution is to fill the vacancy as soon as possible. State statutes may prescribe a quorum.

Voting

A director is deemed to assent to the action taken in a board meeting unless he has objected to the consideration of the question or he has objected to the meeting being held at all, and when he abstains.

Board members should not abstain from voting unless there is a conflict of interest. Abstaining on principle is usually not acceptable when there is an opportunity to vote against the action being considered.

Board members may not vote on board actions by proxy. The principle that the director was elected and is accountable for the action taken prohibits his allowing another to vote in his stead. Condominium boards may not vote by secret ballot.

Check list for board meetings

1. Arrangements made for a room for the meeting
2. Notices sent and posted
3. Agenda written and distributed
4. Supporting documents filed with the secretary
5. A quorum obtained
6. Minutes of previous meeting sent to directors and to employed managers or administrators
7. Equipment on hand
8. ____________________
9. ____________________
10. ____________________

Check list for membership meetings

1. Arrangements made for a room for the meeting
2. Notices sent and posted
3. Proxies and ballots mailed
4. Minutes of previous meeting posted
5. Report of the board completed
6. Preparations completed for registration of proxies and members present in person
7. Preparations completed for elections
8. Equipment on hand
9. ____________________
10. ____________________

Glossary

Glossary

Address the chair • To speak to the presiding officer, using the appropriate title, and asking to be recognized by the Chair to make a motion or to speak in debate.

Adjourn • Adoption of this motion officially closes a meeting.

Adjourned meeting • A continuation of a regular or special meeting at a later date.

Adopt • A motion is adopted when the affirmative vote prevails. A motion is lost when the negative vote prevails.

Agenda • Program; list of items of business to come before the assembly; a list of things to do; order of business that includes call to order and adjournment.

Alternate • A member appointed or elected to take the place of another, such as a convention delegate.

Amend • To change the wording of a motion.

Amendment • A motion that alters a pending motion (Only two amendments may be pending at one time, a Primary amendment and a Secondary amendment.) To amend the bylaws is an incidental main motion.

Announcing the vote • A statement by the Chair giving the result of a vote, action not complete on a motion until the Chair has announced the result of the vote.

Assembly • Members present at a meeting.

Aye vote • The affirmative vote.

Ballot • Usually a written vote; usually a secret vote.

Board • Board of Directors, Trustees, Managers; a group of members elected to act for the association as specified in the bylaws.

Bylaws • A document, adopted by the association, containing the basic rules for governing the group.

Call to order • The official opening of a meeting.

Carried • The same as *adopted.*

Chair • The presiding officer, or the station from which he presides. Mr. Chairman, Madam Chairman. The presiding officer refers to himself as *the Chair.* Other terms that are used to describe the Chair, such as *Chairperson* are legal only when the bylaws so specify, and then are considered substandard.

Committee • One or more persons, appointed or elected, to investigate, report, or take action on particular subjects and questions. There are standing committees and special committees.

Constitution • A document containing the rules that the association has adopted for the management of its affairs.

Consideration • Disposition of a motion that is before the assembly with or without debate.

Consideration by committee • Discussion; examination of referred matter.

Debate • Discussion following the Chair's stating a debatable motion.

Decision • A ruling by the Chair or by the assembly. The parliamentarian advises the Chair, the Chair rules.

Decorum • Appropriateness of conduct in meetings; courtesy and decency towards other members during debate and conduct of business.

Division of the assembly • Call for a rising vote to visually verify a voice vote. This is not a motion for a count of the votes. If a count is desired, a motion to count the vote must be adopted.

Division of the question • A motion consisting of more than one part, each part capable of standing alone, may be divided; that is, debated and voted on separately.

Documents • Association documents may include bylaws, articles of incorporation, declaration of condominium, covenants and restrictions, and others as state statutes specify.

Ex officio • By virtue of the office. The president is not a member *ex officio* of any committee unless such privilege has been granted in special rules or by the bylaws. Temporary officers do not assume *ex officio* duties.

Floor, Obtaining the • A member is recognized by the Chair and granted the privilege of speaking.

General consent • May be called for by the Chair when there does not appear to be opposition to the question, or when there is no objection, also called unanimous consent.

General orders • Questions postponed to a certain day or meeting; amendments.

Germane • Closely related, pertinent. All remarks must be germane to the subject being discussed. A primary amendment must be germane to the pending motion and a secondary amendment must be germane to the primary amendment.

Immediately pending question • The most recent motion introduced upon which no action has been taken.

Lost motion • A motion rejected by vote. A tie vote defeats a motion when a majority vote is required.

Main motion • A motion that brings a matter before the assembly for consideration and action.

Meeting • An assembly of members of a deliberative body to transact business or participate in a program.

Minutes • The official record of business transacted by an association at each regular, special or annual meeting, or convention of delegates.

Motion • A proposal or proposition that the assembly take certain action or express itself as holding certain opinions.

Null and void • Having no legal effect; invalid.

Order of business • The list of official business to come before the assembly, beginning with approval of the minutes and ending at the finish of new business.

Orders of the day • Agenda. Usually the regular order of business, when classes of subjects are taken up in a particular order.

Out of order • In violation of the rules of the association or of the parliamentary authority adopted by the members.

Pending • Undecided or unresolved.

Pending question • A motion that has been stated by the Chair, and upon which no action has been taken.

Preamble • Introduction to a resolution which may be a brief statement of background.

Precedence • Established order of priority of motions; rank.

Prevailing side • The side receiving the greatest number of votes; may be the affirmative side or the negative side.

Previous notice • As the bylaws or adopted rules of order specify; may be given at the previous meeting, by mail to all members, or in the call to meeting.

Pro tem • *Pro tempore.* temporarily; for the time being, a member serving in the absence of the regular officer, chairman, or secretary.

Proxy • A power of attorney or written authorization for a member to act for another.

Limited proxy: will have spaces for the owner to mark yes or no on a question for which notice has been given. A limited proxy is for the designated items only, and not to be used for any other purpose. (Also called a *restricted* proxy.)

General proxy: will have only the spaces to designate an agent. The proxy may be voted in any way the agent chooses.

Putting the question • Taking the vote.

Question • The question is on adopting or rejecting the immediately pending motion.

Quorum •The *Quorum* is the minimum number of members who must be present in order that business may be legally transacted. If the bylaws do not specify otherwise, a quorum is a majority of the members.

Receive • Receive a report; the *hearing* of a report presented either in writing or orally; no action required unless recommendations are included and moved. The reporting member moves the adoption of the *recommended* action. No motion is required to hear a report.

Resolution • A main motion, written in the form of a resolution. It may include a preamble. A resolution should be in writing. Use the term *Resolved* instead of *I move*. The preamble begins with the word *Whereas*.

Rules of order • Written parliamentary rules adopted by the members, usually a parliamentary authority such as *Robert's Rules of Order Newly Revised*.

Second • Indicates that a second member is willing to consider a motion.

Secondary motions • Subsidiary, privileged, and incidental motions.

Seriatim • One after another in a series. To consider seriatim is to consider, debate and amend, section by section or paragraph by paragraph. After all sections have been considered, one vote is taken on the entire document.

Session • A meeting or series of connected meetings such as a convention. An annual meeting and its adjourned meetings are one session.

Speaker • The person who has been assigned the floor.

Special meeting • A meeting called between regular meetings for a special purpose. Notice must be given to all members of the time, place, and purpose of the special meeting. Only business specified in the notice may be transacted.

Special orders • A motion or subject assigned to a certain time and made a special order by a two-thirds vote.

Special rules of order • Rules, adopted by a two-thirds vote after notice, that modify the parliamentary authority.

Standing rules • Relate to administrative details rather than to parliamentary procedure.

Statutes and ordinances • Laws enacted by state and local governments.

Sustain • Uphold the ruling of the Chair.

Tellers • Persons appointed or elected to count the votes and to report to the assembly.

Vote • The expression of the will of the assembly

- Majority vote - more than half the votes cast
- Plurality - the largest number of votes cast
- Two-thirds - at least two thirds of the votes cast
- Tie vote - the same number of negative and affirmative votes
- Unanimous consent - no objection (also called General Consent)
- Unanimous vote - no dissenting votes. This does not mean that everyone voted on the question, but that those on the losing side did not vote at all.

Yield • Accede to, relinquish. Motions yield to other motions of higher rank. A member may not yield any unexpired portion of his time in debate to another member. The right to the floor for debate is not transferable.

QUICK REFERENCE CHART TO DETERMINE A TWO-THIRDS VOTE

Two-thirds (at least two thirds of the votes cast by persons legally entitled to vote, excluding blanks and abstentions, at a regular or properly called meeting at which a quorum is present):

Two-thirds of:

1	is	1	26	is	18	51	is	34	76	is	51
2	is	2	27	is	18	52	is	35	77	is	52
3	is	2	28	is	19	53	is	36	78	is	52
4	is	3	29	is	20	54	is	36	79	is	53
5	is	4	30	is	20	55	is	37	80	is	54
6	is	4	31	is	21	56	is	38	81	is	54
7	is	5	32	is	22	57	is	38	82	is	55
8	is	6	33	is	22	58	is	39	83	is	56
9	is	6	34	is	23	59	is	40	84	is	56
10	is	7	35	is	24	60	is	40	85	is	57
11	is	8	36	is	24	61	is	41	86	is	58
12	is	8	37	is	25	62	is	42	87	is	58
13	is	9	38	is	26	63	is	42	88	is	59
14	is	10	39	is	26	64	is	43	89	is	60
15	is	10	40	is	27	65	is	44	90	is	60
16	is	11	41	is	28	66	is	44	91	is	61
17	is	12	42	is	28	67	is	45	92	is	62
18	is	12	43	is	29	68	is	46	93	is	62
19	is	13	44	is	30	69	is	46	94	is	63
20	is	14	45	is	30	70	is	47	95	is	64
21	is	14	46	is	31	71	is	48	96	is	64
22	is	15	47	is	32	72	is	48	97	is	65
23	is	16	48	is	32	73	is	49	98	is	66
24	is	16	49	is	33	74	is	50	99	is	66
25	is	17	50	is	34	75	is	50	100	is	67

HELPFUL HINTS ON FREQUENTLY USED MOTIONS	
WHAT DO I WANT TO DO?	**MOTION TO USE**
Introduce business. *I move to plant shade trees at the club house.*	Main Motion.
Change or modify a motion before adoption. *I move to amend by inserting "three" before "shade."*	Amend.
Have a few members study or take charge of the matter. *I move to refer the pending motion to the grounds committee to report with a recommendation at the next meeting.*	Commit or Refer.
Postpone the making of a decision. *I move to postpone the question until the next meeting.*	Postpone to a certain time.
Change the rules of debate temporarily on this motion. *I move to limit debate to five minutes on this question.*	Limit or extend limits of debate.
Stop debate and have a vote taken immediately. *I move the previous question (or)* *I move to stop debate.*	Previous question.
Set aside a matter in order to take care of an emergency. *I move to lay the pending motion on the table.*	Lay on the table.
Reopen consideration of a motion that has been tabled. *I move to take from the table the motion relating to planting trees.*	Take from the table.

HELPFUL HINTS ON FREQUENTLY USED MOTIONS	
WHAT DO I WANT TO DO?	**MOTION TO USE**
Protest about noise, heating, ventilation, etc. *I rise to a question of privilege. May we have the window closed to stop the noise?*	Question of privilege.
Have a short intermission. *I move to recess for ten minutes.* *I move to recess until we obtain a quorum.*	Recess.
Close a meeting. *I move to adjourn.*	Adjourn.
Set a time for a continuation of the present meeting. *I move that when we adjourn, we adjourn to meet again at 7 p.m. next Wednesday.*	Fix the time to which to adjourn.
Verify a voice vote. *Division! (or) I call for a division!*	Division of the assembly.
Do something the rules prohibit or take up a question out of proper order. *I move to suspend the rules that prevent our completing action on this item before adjournment.*	Suspend the rules.
Allow members an opportunity to reverse an affirmative vote taken on a motion. *I move to rescind the motion adopted at the last meeting to plant trees at the club house.*	Rescind.
Allow members to take another look at a decision they made. *Having voted on the prevailing side, I move to reconsider the vote on the motion that we plant trees at the club house.*	Reconsider.

Index